WHAT'S THE BIG IDEA?

What's the Big Idea? focuses on the hottest issues
and ideas around. In a nationwide survey, we asked
young people like you to tell us which subjects you
find most intriguing, worrying and exciting.
The books in this series tell you what you need to
know about the top-rated topics.

Books available now:
The Mind
Virtual Reality
Women's Rights

Books coming soon:
Animal Rights
The Environment
Religion
Time and the Universe

We would love to hear what you think. If you
would like to make any comments on this book or
suggestions for future titles, please write to us at:

What's the Big Idea?
Hodder Children's Books
338 Euston Road
London NW1 3BH

For my mother, with love.

*This book is dedicated to the memory of
Lesley-Ann Cameron.*

*The author would like to thank Dr Diana
St.John for her invaluable help and advice.*

Text copyright © Victoria Parker 1996

The right of Victoria Parker to be identified as the author of the
Work has been asserted by her in accordance with the Copyright,
Designs and Patents Act 1988.

Illustrations copyright © Andrew McIntyre 1996

Cover illustration by Jake Abrams

Published by Hodder Children's Books 1996

10 9 8 7 6 5 4 3 2 1

ISBN 0 340 65589 5

A Catalogue record for this book is available from the
British Library.

Printed by Cox and Wyman Ltd, Reading, Berkshire

Hodder Children's Books
A division of Hodder Headline plc
338 Euston Road
London NW1 3BH

WHAT'S THE BIG IDEA?

Women's Rights

Victoria Parker
Illustrated by Andrew McIntyre

Hodder
Children's
Books

a division of Hodder Headline plc

WORRIED? ANXIOUS? CONFUSED?
Just ask Donna...

Dear Donna

I'm fed up with being a girl. Although my brother's only two years younger than me he gets away with doing hardly any housework. Mum's always nagging me to help out more, but she never says anything to him. I'm *sure* it's because he's a boy. How can I make her see that she is being unfair?

Annoyed, Liverpool

Dear Donna

My teachers keep nagging me to work harder at school, but I just can't see the point. Even if I do pass my exams and get a job, I'll only have to give it all up if I have a baby. My mum says you can do both, but I don't see how. If I was a boy it would be different wouldn't it?

Linda, Birmingham

Dear Donna

I'm better at football than all the lads in my class, but my PE teacher won't let me play it in school games lessons. I train really hard at my local club on Saturdays, but at school it doesn't make any difference – all the girls have to play netball! I'm considering a sex change. What do you think?   Sarah 'Maradona' Mitchell,

Dear Donna

My dad says women can't drive. He's always on about it when we're in the car and it really winds me up. He's not right, is he?

Diane, Winchester

Dear Donna

The lads in my class started saying I was ugly, so the other day I wore a bit of make-up and my sister's new short black mini skirt and now they're calling me a tart. I just can't win. What should I do?

Miserable, Woking

Dear Donna

I'm so embarrassed! The other evening I told my dad I'd be back from the Youth Club by 9pm. But I lost track of the time and at 9.30pm he burst in looking for me. I couldn't believe it! I know he was worried about me, but he'd never do that to my brother – he can come back on his own, as long as he's in by 10pm. How can I get a bit more independence?

Frustrated, Belfast

It's sometimes tough for girls. But don't forget that boys have their problems too. Imagine being called 'wet' if you ever cried at anything! Or coping with a part of your body that seems to have a life of its own. And I'm sure that many boys are jealous that we're the ones that can have babies, not them.

But girls also have particular problems that come from being female. And if girls aren't happy it affects boys too. After all, boys grow up with girls, most live with girls, and most eventually have girls of their own. And what kind of dad doesn't want his daughter to have the best chances possible?

Anyway, even though it might not seem like it, it's better to be female now than it has been for a long time! Just read on to find out more.

GIRLS AND BOYS:
HOW DIFFERENT ARE WE?

Think back to the last time you spoke to someone who's about to have a baby … I bet you asked whether they wanted a girl or a boy. The usual answer is that they don't mind what it is, as long as it's healthy, but secretly most people have feelings about which sex they would rather have.
What about you?

But have you ever asked yourself WHY people would rather have one sex than the other? After all, even though they come in different sizes, shapes and colours, all babies - regardless of their sex – are very similar.

Firstly, they're very noisy.

Secondly, they're very smelly.

Thirdly, they leak a lot.

In fact, babies even look the same

This can often lead to embarrassing situations:

Oh, isn't she lovely!

Actually his name is Martin!

But even though most babies look the same and do exactly the same things, many people treat girl and boy babies very differently. Once you know what to look for, this can make it easy to tell which is which. With some basic detective skills and a bit of practice, you need never have to call a baby 'it' again! Here are a couple of pages out of the Alien's Guide to Small Humans to help you.

WHAT'S THE BIG IDEA?

SMALL HUMANS

how to spot those little Earthlings

1. Baby clothes

In the world of baby fashion it's acceptable to dress both boy and girl babies in yellow romper suits, so this may not be much help in working out which is which. But you can bet that if a baby's dressed in anything pink or covered in lace – it's a girl, and if it's dressed in anything blue, or with a picture of a plane, boat or train on it – it's a boy.

2. Toys

Cuddly toys are given to most babies. Again, the colour of the toy may give the game away. Pink fluffy teddies/bunnies/ducks means you're looking at a girl. Blue fluffy teddies/dinosaurs means you're looking at a boy. Boy babies are also more likely to have plastic rattles to shake.

3. The parents

The behaviour of the parents is a dead giveaway. All babies are cuddled, but girls tend to be swung gently back and forth, while boys are jiggled about in a much more energetic manner. Also listen to what the parents say. A girl baby will be called 'beautiful' or 'lovely'. A boy baby will be described as 'a little tinker' or 'a little lad'. A noisy girl baby will be called 'naughty' while a noisy boy baby will be called 'lively' or 'full of life'.

4. If all else fails, peep inside its nappy.

These are only the first of many ways in which girls' and boys' lives are different. Think about what happens as children grow up, and you'll see that it gets easier and easier to spot the differences by watching how girls and boys are treated and how they're expected to behave.

and
there are
Many Many more Differences

But although most people expect girls and boys to be different in these kinds of ways, not everyone feels happy about it! General ideas and expectations about how girls

Not all girls want to …

Think of their appearance

Be caring and gentle..

Some girls would much rather …

Not care how they look

Be competitive

Similarly, not all boys want to …

Wear boys' clothes.

Follow male sports…

Some boys would much rather …

Follow the latest fashions

Try creative activities

and boys should behave (sometimes called 'stereotypes')
can make it difficult for people to do what they want, if
they feel that they don't fit into these broad patterns.

Spend time being quiet,

Discuss boys all the time.

Play physical sports

Have boys as friends

but they may be called 'tomboys' if they do.

Be competitive..... Have girlfriends..

Spend time being quiet.. Have girls as friends...

but they may be called 'sissies' if they do.

In fact, each one of us is unique, with our own thoughts, feelings, abilities, likes and dislikes. SO WHERE HAVE THESE STEREOTYPES ABOUT GIRLS AND BOYS COME FROM? Who first thought 'pink for a girl, blue for a boy'? Who decided that girls and boys should have different interests and play different sports? Why is it said that 'big boys don't cry'? Are girls really made of 'sugar and spice and all things nice'?

Is it perhaps that our brains work differently?

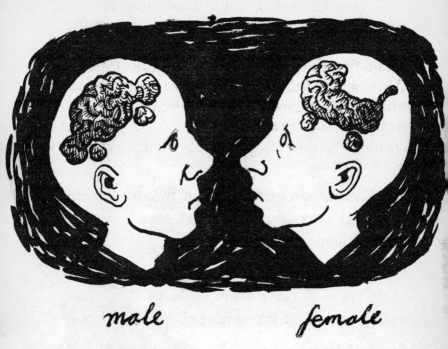

male　　　　　　*female*

Some people think that something inside the female brain makes girls and women more sensitive and 'delicate', more likely to trust their instincts and follow their emotions, more interested in love than sex; and that the female mind is naturally suited to 'arts' academic subjects like literature, languages and social studies.

They think that something inside the male brain gives boys and men 'tougher' characters, making them logical, competitive, aggressive, and more interested in sex than love; and that the male mind is naturally more suited to 'science' academic subjects like chemistry, maths and technology.

But if women's brains make them naturally delicate and sensitive, why is it men who turn away in disgust at changing dirty, smelly nappies? And how come so many more women than men are nurses, dealing daily with blood and gore? And if women are meant to be bad at science subjects, why have there been brilliant women scientists since the earliest times?

For instance:

The Alexandrian mathematician Hypatia (born AD 730) specialized in algebra and mechanics.

Hildegard of Bingen (1098-1179) wrote knowledgeably about medicine and the origin of the universe.

Caroline Herschel (1750-1848) discovered more comets than any other astronomer of her time.

Elizabeth Garrett Anderson (1836-1917) was the first woman to sit the Society of Apothecaries' exam in 1865, and came top, beating all the men.

Physicist Marie Curie (1867-1934) was the first scientist to win two Nobel Prizes.

And if the male brain is meant to be more suited to science and technology, why have there been so many great male painters, actors and writers?

If men are naturally 'tougher', suited to protecting and looking after women, why is it that all over the world women spend every day looking after men?

And a lot of cultures believe that men are just as emotional as women. Men in Mediterranean and Arab countries show their emotions much more than reserved British chaps.

fig A

fig B

If men's brains are meant to make them better leaders and more aggressive than women, why have there always been fierce and strong warrior women who have led powerful peoples? Here are just a few of them.

WHO AM I?

1   I ruled Egypt in the 15th century BC. I was called Pharoah, statues and pictures show me wearing a beard and I built a temple in the Valley of the Kings. Who am I?

2   I was Queen of the Iceni in Britain around 60 AD and led my tribe against the invading Romans. I sacrificed any Roman women I captured to the goddess Andraste, whose name meant 'She Who Is Invincible'. Who am I?

3   I was a queen in 7th century Africa who recaptured the ancient city of Carthage from the Arabs. The landscape of Tunisia still bears the scars of my wars. Who am I?

4   I ruled one third of present day France between 1122 and 1204. I established a court which was an important centre for culture and the arts, and I went to the Crusades. Who am I?

5   In 1346, when the Scots attacked the English at the Battle of Neville's Cross, County Durham, I raised the army which defeated them. Who am I?

6   I led an army that liberated Orleans, France, from the English in 1429, and was later burnt at the stake as a witch. Who am I?

7   I was a Nigerian warrior queen of the 16th century who took a lover in every town I conquered. I beheaded each one the morning after. Who am I?

8   I led a rebel force in India in the 1980s to fight for the rights of women and the lower castes, and as a result spent eleven years in gaol as a political prisoner. Who am I?

1 Hatshepsut   2 Boudicca/Boadicea   3 Kahina   4 Eleanor of Aquitaine   5 Philippa of Hainault   6 Amina of Hausaland   7 Joan of Arc   8 Phoolan Devi, 'the Bandit Queen'

What about our bodies? Do they make us different? As girls and boys, our physical differences aren't all that noticeable. But between the ages of about 10 and 14, female and male hormones get to work on us. After this, it's hard to ignore the fact that women's and men's bodies are different.

EARTHLINGS: what their bodies tell us!

female

As breasts are such an obvious sexual sign, it's clear that the female is designed first and foremost to attract the male. And, as it's the females rather than the males who can have babies, it follows that all females want babies and that all females have a natural instinct for looking after them!

Male

As the male is designed to have less body fat than the female, and they find it easier to put on muscle, most males are naturally stronger than females. It therefore follows that the Male is better than the female!

Ha HO He Ho! Ha!

You don't have to be Einstein to work out that women and men are designed differently so humans can have babies. And most other living things come in female and male varieties for the same reason. But it's all too easy to look at the female and male body and make general judgements.

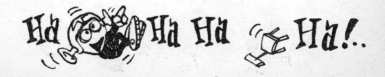

Ha Ha Ha Ha!..

No!

OK, it's hard not to notice breasts, as they're stuck on to the front of your chest. And it's true that a lot of boys focus on them as a sign of sexual attractiveness and find it hard to notice anything else about us. But just because we have breasts, it doesn't mean that women are sex objects. The biological purpose of breasts is to feed babies.

And just because it's only women who can have babies, it doesn't mean that all women want them, or that all

women are naturally good at looking after them. My friend Simon has got five younger sisters, and he's much better with babies than I am! I think that how you feel about starting your own family has a lot to do with what your family life was like when you were growing-up. I don't think it's much to do with natural instinct.

And I don't agree either!

I know women naturally have more body fat than men, but look at women body builders - they've got more muscles than I'll ever have! And I reckon women's bodies have to be pretty tough in order to cope with having babies - I wouldn't like all that painful stuff! Don't women generally live longer than men, too?

Anyway, even if most men are physically stronger than most women, it doesn't necessarily follow that men's brains are better. You don't have to have a strong body to have a very good brain. My next-door-neighbour can't get out of her wheelchair, but she's a university lecturer!

By the way, can anyone tell me why boys have nipples?

It's obvious that our different bodies limit what we can and can't do physically, and this means we have different experiences. For example, because women can have babies and men can't, it has to be true that life as a woman is different from life as a man.

But there are many things other than our bodies that make us what we are, such as our different families and friends, where we live, what we're taught at school, our likes and dislikes and our memories. We are all individuals who have different talents, strengths and weaknesses, and are good and bad at different things. So it's just not logical to split everyone up into two broad groups and say that men are better than women (or vice versa).

But if you look around you, you'll see that all over the world there are more successful and powerful men than there are women. The world's top ten richest men have more money than the world's top ten richest women. There are more men in governments than women. There are more men making big business decisions in companies than women. There are more male than female university lecturers, TV and film producers, surgeons, engineers and sports professionals. So, if we're all individuals, equally capable of success, regardless of whether we are female or male – why is the world like this? And has it always been the same?

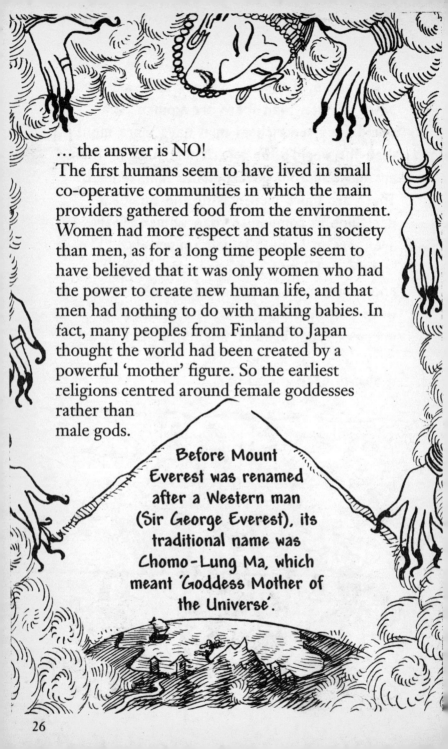

… the answer is NO!

The first humans seem to have lived in small co-operative communities in which the main providers gathered food from the environment. Women had more respect and status in society than men, as for a long time people seem to have believed that it was only women who had the power to create new human life, and that men had nothing to do with making babies. In fact, many peoples from Finland to Japan thought the world had been created by a powerful 'mother' figure. So the earliest religions centred around female goddesses rather than male gods.

Before Mount Everest was renamed after a Western man (Sir George Everest), its traditional name was Chomo-Lung Ma, which meant 'Goddess Mother of the Universe'.

Men probably started to become more important when people invented weapons and began hunting as well as gathering their food. Men would have been good at hunting because of their upper body strength. But even so, historical evidence suggests that women were capable of being just as fierce and aggressive as men – if not more so.

Coatlicue, the Aztec Goddess of Earth and Fire had a necklace of human hearts and hands and a skirt made from Live Snakes!

Ammut, the Egyptian demon who ate the hearts of Sinners, had a Crocodile's head, a Cat's body and a Hippo's bottom!

Most early deities worshipped for hunting, war, battle and victory seem to have been female rather than male, such as Badb, the Irish goddess of war; Korrawi, the Tamil goddess of battle and victory; and Diana, the Roman goddess of hunters. And many demons and monsters were also thought to be female. Their frightening natures and appearances are very different from today's ideals of beauty and gentleness!

The Greek Goddess Lamia was a Vampire who abducted children!

Medusa the Gorgon, turned people to Stone if they looked at her!

28

But around 4000 BC, men began to overpower women, forcing them to take second place in society. This was the beginning of 'patriarchy' - the male-dominated world we know today. By the time of most of the great ancient civilizations, men had restricted women's lives in many ways. In ancient Egypt, few jobs were open to women; the Romans killed so many girl babies at birth (because boys were preferred) that they ended up with a shortage of suitable wives; and women in Athens - together with slaves - weren't even considered 'citizens'.

Many men began to insist that children carried their father's family name rather than their mother's. And they started to treat women as their property, to be bought and sold through marriage.

Many cultures started to make a bride's family pay a 'dowry' (a sum of money, or the rights to property or land) to the new husband. Obviously, families would try to obtain a bride with the largest possible dowry for their son, so women from poor families had very little choice over who they could marry, or whether they could get married at all.

Royal women too, often had very little say over whom they married, as the marriage was often used for political purposes, to build links between foreign countries. For instance, Isabella of Valois (1387-1410) was only eight years old when she was married to Richard II of England.

Think about a traditional English wedding today and you'll see that in many ways it still follows these ideas. In the marriage service, the bride is 'given away' by her father to her new 'owner', the groom, whom she often promises to 'obey'. And at the wedding reception, only the men usually make speeches. All the women - even the bride herself - are expected to remain silent.

In medieval times, men held power at all levels - whether rich or poor. At court, the king and knights expected noble ladies to behave with perfect obedience and gentleness, as models of virtue and purity. Locally, the Lord of the Manor was entitled to a night with a new bride before her wedding night with her husband. And, by law, a man was the master of his wife and children, while she was classed on the same level as lunatics and lepers.

By the 14th century, most European women were prevented from having anything more than a very basic education. You may think that no school sounds like heaven, but it meant that women were unable to have jobs and incomes of their own. Even when women worked as midwives and wise women (jobs that didn't require book learning), people who had always turned to them for medical advice and herbal cures now began to accuse them of being witches and devil worshippers, drowning them or burning them at the stake.

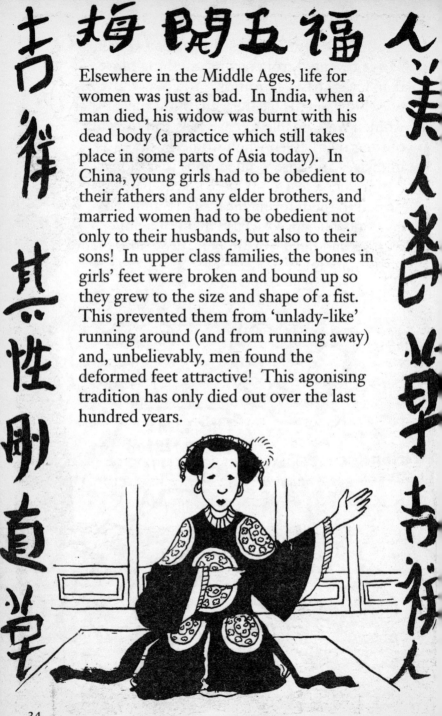

Elsewhere in the Middle Ages, life for women was just as bad. In India, when a man died, his widow was burnt with his dead body (a practice which still takes place in some parts of Asia today). In China, young girls had to be obedient to their fathers and any elder brothers, and married women had to be obedient not only to their husbands, but also to their sons! In upper class families, the bones in girls' feet were broken and bound up so they grew to the size and shape of a fist. This prevented them from 'unlady-like' running around (and from running away) and, unbelievably, men found the deformed feet attractive! This agonising tradition has only died out over the last hundred years.

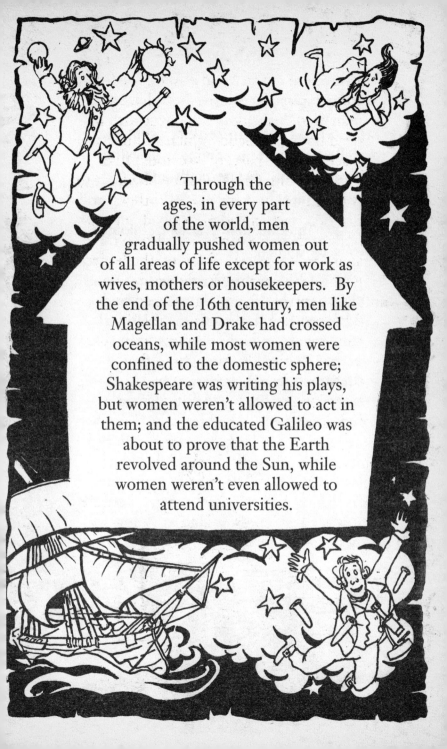

Through the ages, in every part of the world, men gradually pushed women out of all areas of life except for work as wives, mothers or housekeepers. By the end of the 16th century, men like Magellan and Drake had crossed oceans, while most women were confined to the domestic sphere; Shakespeare was writing his plays, but women weren't allowed to act in them; and the educated Galileo was about to prove that the Earth revolved around the Sun, while women weren't even allowed to attend universities.

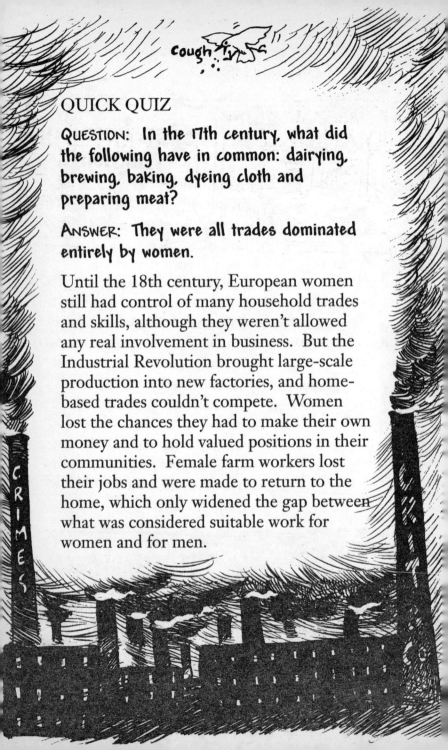

cough

QUICK QUIZ

QUESTION: In the 17th century, what did the following have in common: dairying, brewing, baking, dyeing cloth and preparing meat?

ANSWER: They were all trades dominated entirely by women.

Until the 18th century, European women still had control of many household trades and skills, although they weren't allowed any real involvement in business. But the Industrial Revolution brought large-scale production into new factories, and home-based trades couldn't compete. Women lost the chances they had to make their own money and to hold valued positions in their communities. Female farm workers lost their jobs and were made to return to the home, which only widened the gap between what was considered suitable work for women and for men.

Now imagine you're a woman living in the 19th century. How do you like it?

If you're upper class, your husband is rich enough to support you, so there is normally nothing for you to do except sit uselessly indoors. You are virtually a prisoner in your own home, with no rights to earn your own income or to own property.

In fact, you are legally your husband's property, along with your children, and anything you owned before you got married. Your husband can do whatever he likes with you; if you disagree with him he can legally beat you or say you're mad and lock you up.

If you're a middle class woman and you're determined to try to keep some freedom, you'll have to stay single. This means you'll have to work to support yourself, but very few jobs are thought to be 'proper' for you, such as a lady's companion or a children's governess. Both these jobs are poorly paid, overcrowded and only one step up from being a household servant. If you do eventually decide to get married, you'll have to give up your job.

If you're a working class woman, you'll probably have become a domestic servant at around 13 or 14, separated from your family and living a slave-like existence under a tyrannical employer. If you're less fortunate, you'll be working long hours in a badly-lit, cold and dirty factory or sweatshop for dreadful pay. If you're even more unlucky, you will have been forced to work down a mine, dragging cartloads of coal through tiny shafts. You may even have found that prostitution is your best bet for making enough money to keep yourself alive.

In the early 19th century, it looked as if things were never going to get better for women. But throughout history, time and time again, oppressed people have rebelled. And women weren't going to put up with their situation for much longer. Women were about to fight back.

MOVEMENT FOR WOMEN'S RIGHTS

Why did it take so long for women to realise men were keeping them in second place? Didn't anyone before the Victorians try to do something about it?

Because people had been brainwashed for centuries into thinking that men were superior, most women never thought to question the way things were. From time to time, individuals, such as Christine de Pisan in the 15th century and Bathsua Makin in the 17th century, had suggested that it might be useful to educate girls, but learning was only available to nuns. And, though many girls fled to convents to escape from the difficulties of outside life, no one had pointed out that it was the domination of society by men which was preventing women from living full lives.

But the 18th century was an exciting time of widespread change. Across Europe, the gap between the few rich people in power and the masses living in terrible poverty had grown too large to bear. Even the middle classes were fed up with the excesses of the nobility and wanted change. In England, people had begun to question whether the noble classes had the right to rule the country, and in France the working class rose up in violent revolution, sweeping away the old royal family, who were long out of touch with the lives and needs of the common people.

Give us food! We're starving!

We want education for all! Banish ignorance!

We want to have a say in government! Down with the monarchy!

In this new atmosphere of change, when the poor had begun to think they were entitled to the same as the rich, two women dared to think for the first time that women might be entitled to the same as men.

In France, demonstrations by working women were the driving force behind much of the Revolution. But they weren't just demanding better conditions in general. French women wanted specific things for themselves too. In 1791, Olympe de Gouge (1748-93) published a book called *The Declaration of the Rights of Women*, demanding equal rights for women in law, government and education.

We want the right to vote!
To own property!
To divorce our husbands!
To hold important public jobs!

At the same time in England, Mary Wollstonecraft (1759-97) wrote *A Vindication of the Rights of Woman*, published in 1792. Tragically, she died in childbirth. But her ideas were a vital starting point for the growth of an organised movement for women's full rights as human beings, later known as 'feminism'.

Women aren't naturally inferior to men. Men have made us like this by denying us education and keeping us shut up indoors. And there aren't special female and male qualities, only human ones. I'm sure that with the same opportunities, women are just as capable of achieving success as men. And if girls were educated properly, they'd not only be of use to society, they'd also have the freedom that comes from earning your own living.

In the early years of the 19th century there was a great backlash against any such revolutionary ideas, and it was hard to get people to listen to Mary Wollstonecraft's views. Many people were horrified by her book, even calling her 'a hyena in petticoats'.

It wasn't until much later on that women did anything practical about Mary Wollstonecraft's ideas. In England, the 'Ladies of Langham Place' were a small but determined group of women including Barbara Bodichon (1827-91), Emily Davies (1830-1921) and Elizabeth Garrett Anderson (1836-1917) – the first British woman doctor – who opened offices at 19 Langham Place, London, to fight for women's rights. Besides organising petitions, they launched *The English Woman's Journal*, which not only discussed issues such as women's health, education, work and legal rights, but also demanded that women be given the vote.

In America, another struggle that helped women's rights was the fight against slavery. As in Europe, white women had no rights. But the situation for black women was even worse. Torn away from their families and made the legal property of a white master, they were in twofold slavery: firstly because of their colour, secondly, because of their sex.

Many protesters against black slavery also found themselves speaking out for women's rights, such as Sojourner Truth (1797-83), herself an escaped slave.

THAT MAN OVER THERE SAYS WOMEN NEED TO BE HELPED INTO CARRIAGES AND LIFTED OVER DITCHES AND TO HAVE THE BEST PLACE EVERYWHERE, NOBODY EVER HELPS ME INTO CARRIAGES OR OVER PUDDLES OR GIVES ME THE BEST PLACE AND AIN'T I A WOMAN? I COULD WORK AS MUCH AND EAT AS MUCH AS A MAN, WHEN I COULD GET IT, AND BEAR THE LASH AS WELL, AND AIN'T I A WOMAN? I HAVE BORNE THIRTEEN CHILDREN AND SEEN MOST OF 'EM SOLD OFF INTO SLAVERY AND WHEN I CRIED OUT WITH MY WOMAN'S GRIEF... NONE BUT JESUS HEARD ME — AND AIN'T I A WOMAN?

QUICK QUIZ?

Why were the American Anti-Slavery protestors Lucretia Mott (1793-1850) & Elizabeth Cady Stanton (1815-1902) enraged when they attended the International Anti-Slavery Convention in England in 1840?

Answer

They were made to sit behind a curtain because they were women!

It was obvious to Lucretia and Elizabeth that women had as much need as slaves for an organized movement to push for their freedom. They drew up the *Seneca Falls Declaration of Sentiments*, stating that all women and men are created equal, and held the first women's rights convention in a tiny chapel at 10 am on the 19th July 1848. Together with Susan B Anthony and Lucy Stone, Elizabeth went on to organize meetings all over America to campaign for women's rights and, above all, the vote.

But it wasn't only women who stood up for female rights in the 19th century; a couple of brave new thinkers were in fact men.

In 1825 William Thompson said that women were prisoners in their homes, but he was ridiculed for this view. He supported Mary Wollstonecraft's ideas and wrote a book on fair treatment and equal laws for women and men.

In *The Subjection of Women* (1869), John Stuart Mill argued that women deserved equal rights. And Friedrich Engels (1820-95) tried to use historical evidence in his book, *The Origins of the Family, Private Property and the State*, to show that women hadn't always been inferior to men.

Men have animal passions and appetites for sex, drinking and gambling! Women don't need these things, so they're much better than men.

And not everyone within the new women's movement agreed all the time, either. There was a new form of feminist thinking in the 1870s and 80s which believed that women weren't in fact equal with men - but that women were better!

No! Women have just as healthy an appetite for sex as men, and our behaviour should be judged by the same standards. When drinking was prohibited in America, it didn't make any difference to how men treated us. Change will only come by women winning the vote.

So Why Was Getting the Vote So Important?

 Without the vote, women had no say over who governed the country and they couldn't be in the Government themselves. All the power was in the hands of men who didn't consider women's point of view.

 As women had no power to vote, Parliament had no reason to listen to them. The only way MPs would pay attention to what women wanted was if they had to rely on women's voting support as well as men's to stay in power.

 The fact that women couldn't vote clearly showed that the underlying attitude of society was that women were second class citizens. Winning the right to vote would be a vital step towards equality with men.

In 1893 New Zealand gave the vote to women, closely followed by South Australia in 1894. Spurred on by this, Millicent Fawcett set up the National Union of Women's Suffrage Societies (NUWSS) in Britain in 1897. Its members (the Suffragists) petitioned Parliament, wrote pamphlets and organised marches to demonstrate for votes for women.

But in 1903 Emmeline Pankhurst decided that the only way women were going to get the vote was to fight for it - literally! She formed the Women's Social and Political Union (WSPU) with her daughters Christabel and Sylvia, and women all over the country flocked to join. They called themselves Suffragettes.

We had many violent clashes with the police. Led by Christabel, we disrupted political meetings, hounded MPs and tried repeatedly to get into the House of Commons. On 'Black Friday' in November 1910, Fifty women were seriously injured and two died. We were continually arrested but even then managed to continue our protest by going on hunger strike. The police didn't know what to do! In 1911, Prime Minister Asquith promised to give the vote to women who owned property. But he did nothing about it after the new King's coronation in 1912. So, furious, we smashed windows, damaged property and blew up public buildings with home-made bombs. But then, in 1914, the war with Germany started and people's attention switched elsewhere.

"YOUR COUNTRY NEEDS **YOU**"

But World War I (1914-18) was a turning point for women. More and more men were called up to fight and, by 1915, women were told to take over their jobs. They set to work building ships and aircraft, working in metal foundries, on the railways and the buses, in offices, banks and the civil service. By 1917 women were needed in the Forces too, in jobs such as clerical work, cooking and driving. By the end of the war, the government could no longer ignore women and, on 17th February 1918, an Act was passed giving women aged 30 and over the vote, as long as they owned property.

Slowly, all over the world, women won the fight to be able to vote, without any property, class or race restrictions.

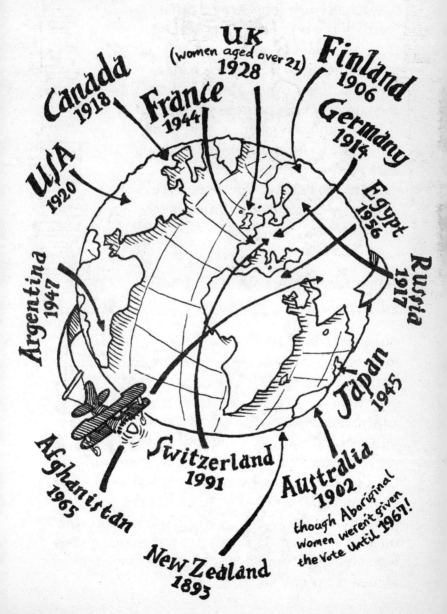

Canada 1918
France 1944
UK (women aged over 21) 1928
Finland 1906
Germany 1914
USA 1920
Egypt 1956
Argentina 1947
Russia 1917
Japan 1945
Afghanistan 1965
Switzerland 1991
Australia 1902
though Aboriginal women weren't given the vote until 1967!
New Zealand 1893

So surely winning the vote meant that the fight for women's rights was over? Wrong! It was only the first victory in a long struggle that is still going on today. After several thousand years of oppression, women weren't going to be able to change men's attitudes overnight. Winning the vote was vital because without it, there was no way women were going to be able to have the power to change society: the way they were treated and expected to behave. But there were, and still are, many other hurdles to overcome.

Watch the fifth hurdle, it's a bit wobbly!

choices
independent
Prospects
equality
sex
home
Jobs
education
VOTE
2

What images come to mind when you think of Britain in the 1920s? Flapper girls? The Charleston? Cocktail parties and cigarette holders? In fact, life for most women in Britain in the 1920s was still very hard.

Single middle class girls are the first generation of liberated women. And from 1928 we can vote if we're over 21. But even though we can be shop assistants, teachers, nurses and secretaries, we're much worse paid than men, these jobs aren't very well thought of, and we have to give them up the day we get married. And it's very difficult to force your way into a university as people can't understand why women need to be educated.

The only choice for single working class girls is domestic service, just like before the war. Us married women are desperate to keep working in our wartime jobs, but they've sent us all back home! One in three of us lost our husbands fighting, so if we can't work, how can we support ourselves? And the cost of living has doubled since before the war! Marie Stopes' book <u>Married Love</u> says that women have as much right as men to enjoy sex. But there's nowhere for us to go for birth control, so we're trapped into having large families when we can't afford to feed and clothe them. At least the new laws mean we can now divorce our husbands for being unfaithful, as well as the other way around.

In the 1930s, things were worse. Many young women couldn't find a husband because so many men had been killed in the war. But single women had a hard time supporting themselves because there was a shortage of jobs. Most people were hard-up, and women's health became a national problem as women spent what little they had on their families and neglected themselves.

With the vote won, the women's rights movement turned to improving women's lives within the family. Feminist Eleanor Rathbone entered Parliament in 1929 as one of the first women MPs. She campaigned for Family Allowance payments; not only to give women financial help, but also to give them recognition and respect for their work as mothers.

In World War II (1939-45), women were again needed for all kinds of war work, and in some cases were even conscripted like the men. But at the end of the war in 1945 they were told to down tools and return quietly to their kitchens. However, as the economy quickly improved, women began to go back to work part time.

WE LIKE PART TIME WORK BECAUSE WE CAN EARN MONEY AS WELL AS HAVING TIME FOR OUR FAMILIES

THEY DON'T REALISE THAT US BOSSES LIKE IT BECAUSE WE CAN PAY WOMEN LESS AND GIVE THEM THE MINDLESS JOBS MEN DON'T WANT.

..BUT THEY WON'T LET US BACK INTO THE 'MEN'S JOBS' WE DID SO WELL DURING THE WAR.

AND IT'S IMPOSSIBLE FOR US TO GET TOP JOBS BECAUSE OF THE ATTITUDE THAT WOMEN ONLY WORK FOR EXTRAS IN THE HOUSE

In the 50s, working married women faced a large amount of opposition. Wartime nurseries closed, male psychologists said that staying at home was the only way to bring up a healthy, well-balanced baby, and advertisers sold women the luxury of staying at home with new household appliances like washing machines and fridges. The fairytale marriage of Hollywood film star, Grace Kelly, to the Prince of Monaco in 1955 was held up as an ideal all women should aim for. But one clear voice who spoke up for women's rights was the French woman, Simone de Beauvoir. In her book, *The Second Sex* (1949), she insisted that men were turning women into *their* idea of what women should be, and that women should fight back for equal treatment and opportunities.

In the 1960s, the American Betty Friedan put her finger on 'the problem that has no name' in her book, *The Feminine Mystique*. More girls than ever were going to college and living independent lives. But even after studying, when they married, they were expected to stay at home and be model housewives. They may have had comfortable home lives, but they just didn't feel satisfied!

Women began to meet in groups to discuss what they called women's liberation. They argued that both parents should be responsible for bringing up children, not just women. And that men should do more inside the home so women could do more outside it.

Quick Quiz

Did women's libbers really burn their bras?

Women protested outside the 'Miss America' beauty contest in Atlanta City in 1968 by throwing things like false eyelashes, under-wired bras and dishcloths into a dustbin. They felt these symbolised the restrictive nature of male expectations of women. Some people say that they then set fire to them. Others say that journalists added this detail just to make the women appear ridiculous.

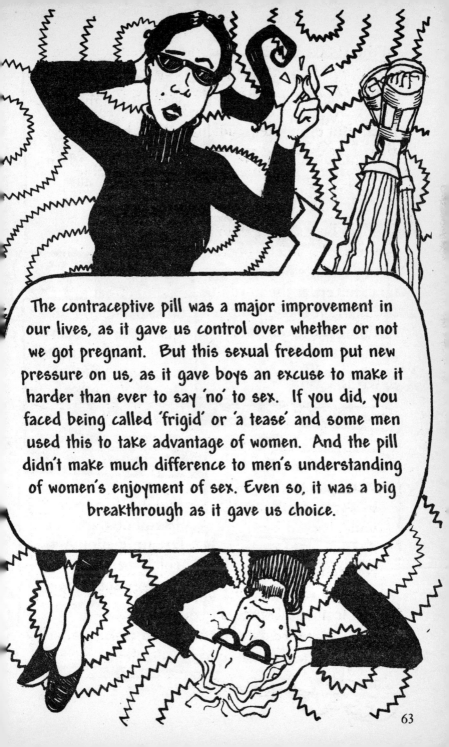

The contraceptive pill was a major improvement in our lives, as it gave us control over whether or not we got pregnant. But this sexual freedom put new pressure on us, as it gave boys an excuse to make it harder than ever to say 'no' to sex. If you did, you faced being called 'frigid' or 'a tease' and some men used this to take advantage of women. And the pill didn't make much difference to men's understanding of women's enjoyment of sex. Even so, it was a big breakthrough as it gave us choice.

Equal pay was another big issue in the late 60s. Women had always been paid less than men for doing the same, or equivalent, work.

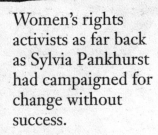

Women's rights activists as far back as Sylvia Pankhurst had campaigned for change without success.

In 1968, women workers at the Ford plant in Dagenham brought the factory to a standstill by striking for equal pay.

This sparked off other equal pay strikes up and down the country, and a huge rally was organised in 1969 in Trafalgar Square.

But it took two committed women to make real changes in the workplace.

And, in 1975, Nancy Sear piloted the Sex Discrimination Act, which made it illegal to refuse someone a job because of their sex.

In 1970, Barbara Castle pushed through the Equal Pay Act which demanded that women and men were paid equally for doing the same work.

Women's groups sprang up in most towns and the first national meeting of the Women's Liberation Movement in the UK took place at Ruskin College, Oxford in 1970. The movement had some very different ideas from those of earlier feminists. Rather than wanting to be the same as men, the Women's Liberation Movement demanded the freedom to be women. It argued that women's feelings about themselves and their home lives weren't just emotions, but also important political issues.

We need to face the fact that women are different from men. But being different isn't the same as being inferior.

We need to stand up for our experiences as women.

We don't want to be 'honorary men', we want to be important as women in our own right.

In the 70s, there was an explosion of ideas and campaigns by the Women's Liberation Movement, who realised that women often had very different problems to men. For example, many women with violent husbands couldn't escape because they had no money and nowhere to go. In 1971, Erin Pizzey set up the first refuge for battered women, and the Women's Aid Foundation went on to set up 150 more, helping nearly 12,000 women and 21,000 children by 1978.

But at the end of the 70s, some members of the Women's Liberation Movement started calling for a feminist revolution, for a war against men instead of a war for women's rights. They began to blame men for everything, making women out to be victims, with no power over their own lives. Others didn't agree, and by the end of the 1980s, after many arguments, the Women's Rights Movement fell apart altogether.

So did this mean that there was no longer the need for a women's rights movement after the 1970s? Unfortunately, no!

In 1979 Britain elected its first woman Prime Minister, Margaret Thatcher. It was a huge and inspiring break-through to have a woman leading the country. But even though women made up more than half of the voters, there was a total of only 19 women in Parliament compared to 616 men!

Without a widespread women's movement to push to improve this situation, a small organisation was set up in 1980 called the '300 Group', with the aim of getting 300 women MPs into the House of Commons. 'Emily's List' is a group today in America with the same aim of getting a fair representation of women into Parliament.

Power & Success

Miners' wives stood on picket lines with their striking husbands, in support of the trade unions.

Nurses went on strike for the first time ever to protest about a lack of funding in the Health Service.

Thousands of women camped outside the Greenham Common Air Base to demonstrate against American missiles being based in Britain.

Mrs Thatcher herself wasn't sympathetic to women's demands for rights, and her Conservative Government did many things which undermined the achievements of the women's liberation campaigners of the 1970s. A job shortage meant that many women couldn't find work, and cutbacks in spending closed social services women depended on, such as nurseries, which put more pressure on women in the home. Different groups of women banded together to protest against the government's actions and national policies.

Today, women still have no organized movement to support them. It has been only one hundred years or so since women started to demand rights, and attitudes held for around 6000 years die hard. Also, many men feel that women's achievements threaten their own importance, so women often face opposition when trying to take advantage of their new opportunities.

How do you think men should fit into today's society?

When I get married, I'll earn enough money for my wife to stay at home and look after the kids.

But I think both the man and the woman should go out to work, and should share looking after the kids and the work around the house between them. Kids need to have a father around just as much as a mother.

I know some men are househusbands, but I couldn't imagine staying at home while my wife went out to work. I'd do a bit of hoovering and washing up, but facing housework and screaming kids every day would drive me mad!

It's not just men who are confused by their changing role in society. Women now feel they should be able to 'have it all', to have both satisfying jobs and home lives, as men do. But things haven't yet changed enough to give women the support they need to do this.

How do you think women should fit into today's society?

Girls and boys are largely given the same education at school, so really we ought to have the same opportunities.

Yes, women should be able to stay at home if they want, but there's no reason now why girls shouldn't be able to do whatever jobs they like.

But why bother trying for a good job anyway? You only have to give it all up to have a baby. Men don't help enough around the house still, so it's impossible for women to have a decent career and bring up a family.

Girls today undoubtedly have many more choices than their great-grandmothers, grandmothers and mothers. But is life really that much easier when they grow up?

Drop Mel off at school, take Gemma to the child-minder, don't forget board report, ask Jayne to cancel tomorrow's meeting, pick Jim's suit up from the dry-cleaner's, go to aerobics, call Mum to see if she's OK, test Mel on her spellings, Sue and Dave coming for supper, do the washing-up, don't forget the dog food...AAAAAAARRRRRGGGGGGHHHHH!

WHERE DO WE GO FROM HERE?

Some people think that the fight for women's rights has been largely won. But if we look closely at women's lives all over the world, it's clear that women still have many problems *because* they are women. And as many men feel threatened by the advances women have made, it's often harder than ever for women to win further rights.

It's dirty work, but somebody's got to do it! Since time began, childcare and housework are vital tasks that have needed doing routinely every day in order for the human race to survive. But because these chores don't make money, they are usually not thought of as 'work', and the people who do them – generally women – aren't given the respect they deserve. Nowadays, if a woman chooses to stay at home with her family, she often feels guilty that she isn't doing more, calling herself 'just a housewife'.

I've had a terrible day! I'm going to sit in front of the telly.

At least you work from 9 till 5. I can't ever clock off!

It's true that most men no longer feel like 'sissies' if they do the hoovering, load up the washing machine or cook a meal. But though they do these tasks from time to time, the ultimate responsibility for making sure that the household runs smoothly, for taking time off work when children are sick, and for caring for elderly relatives usually still falls on women – whether they work or not.

Mum still asks me rather than my brother to help with the dusting, ironing and washing up. And Mum now does all the traditionally 'male' jobs around the house too, such as DIY and maintaining the cars.

Families in which the woman goes out to work while the man stays at home are still very rare, and even when dads take on the responsibility of bringing up their children on their own, female friends or family may treat them as if they're not able to cope, flocking around to help out. Not all dads welcome this, of course! Many single dads complain that they feel excluded by 'mother and toddler' groups and by practicalities such as baby-changing rooms being in women's toilets.

Working conditions usually make it very difficult for people to cope with both jobs and families. Most companies don't allow working flexible hours, so it's impossible to time shifts to coincide with school hours. There's also very little childcare provided by the government: in 1995 it was reported that the UK had the worst state provision of childcare in Europe, jointly with Portugal.

Only a few companies run nurseries, so for many people the cost of childcare is more than they earn anyway! And it's still usually women rather than men who compromise on their working lives in order to be available for their children. In the UK in 1995, though more women are in paid employment than men, 90% of all part-time, low-paid and low-status workers are women.

Childcare is not the only problem that working women have to deal with. Women have other problems in the workplace which men don't often face, such as being judged on their appearance rather than their performance.

President Clinton's new slicked back hair-do and dashing designer suit wowed world leaders at today's summit meeting.

And women's and men's behaviour at work is often judged by very different standards:

It's just not good enough. You'll have to start again.

ASSERTIVE

AGGRESSIVE

Although women and men are now meant to have equal opportunities at work, this isn't necessarily the case. Old attitudes die hard, and it can be just as tough for a girl who wants to be a plumber or a policewoman as it is for a boy who wants to be a secretary or a midwife.

People who take on jobs traditionally done by the other sex, often face a lot of teasing from their colleagues, and sometimes even bullying or harassment.

Some companies actively try and recruit more women, so they get a fair balance of women and men in their workforce. But other employers might decide not to hire or promote a woman if they think she might soon choose to get pregnant and take time off to start a family. Because this kind of prejudice is now illegal, companies make all sorts of excuses about why women are not being employed or promoted, and it's often very hard for women to prove it's just because they're female.

Many jobs traditionally done by women, such as teaching, nursing and secretarial work, are much worse paid than jobs traditionally done by men, such as banking and accountancy. And many women who do the same jobs as men feel that payrises and promotions are more likely to go to their male counterparts than themselves, because the attitude still exists that it's the man who has to support the family, not the woman.

Thank you for answering my questions about new Supersuds washing powder. Can I just ask the job of the head of the household, please? What do you do for a living, sir?

I'm the head of the household, actually.

Women *are* succeeding in breaking through to top positions at work, but there is still a long way to go. In the UK in 1995, women made up less than 16% of all managers and less than 3% of directors on the boards of major UK companies. Until women achieve these positions of influence within the workplace, attitudes to childcare, working hours and working conditions won't change. In 1995, Britain had the worst maternity and paternity leave arrangements in Europe. And while women who go back to work full-time after having a baby are often called 'career women', and made to feel guilty that they've 'abandoned' their children, there's no such thing as a 'career man'.

My First P.C.

Even in professions which centre on traditionally 'female' activities, women have a lot of ground to make up. In 1989, 75% of the UK's teachers were women, but only 15% of these were headteachers. And in 1993, out of 1,247 academic staff at Oxford University, only 176 were women.

Day in and day out, all over the world, all through history, it has been women's responsibility to clothe and feed their families. But most of the top chefs and, until recently, most of the top fashion designers, are men, not women!

The field of science and technology has always been difficult for women to break into. Denied education, women interested in science had either to teach themselves or help scientific brothers or fathers in their work. The scientific achievements of many women have either been overlooked or credited to men, so there are few well-known female scientists for girls to follow as role models. Most girls are encouraged to be aware today that scientific jobs are open to them, but many are put off by the fact that science is still very much male-dominated. In 1995, only 2% of science professors in the UK were women.

Have you heard of these women who were leading lights in the field of science, despite these difficulties?

1) The medical texts I wrote in the 11th century were so good that many historians refused to believe I wasn't a man. Who am I?

2) In the 19th century I disguised myself as a man in order to study at Edinburgh School of Medicine and was only discovered to be a woman at my death. Who am I?

3) I lived in the 17th century and wrote a very influential book called 'Principles of the Most Ancient and Modern Philosophy'. After my death, my name was deliberatedly removed from the title page, so everyone assumed my book was written by a man. Who am I?

4) I lived in the 18th century and introduced innoculations against smallpox in England. Who am I?

5) The mechanical cotton gin is believed to have been invented by Eli Whitney in 1793, but it was my idea, I encouraged him to build it and I helped him to improve the design. Who am I?

6) In the early 19th century I wrote a series of science books, beginning with one called 'Conversations on Chemistry, intended more especially for the Female Sex'. My ideas inspired Michael Faraday, who was famous for his research into electricity. Who am I?

1) Trotula   2) Dr Miranda (James) Barry   3) Lady Anne Conway   4) Lady Mary Wortley Montagu   5) Catherine Greene   6) Jane Marcet

7) I revolutionized nursing and public health, opening a school for Nurses at St Thomas's Hospital in London in 1860. As I was single, worked outside the home, and acted on my own ideas, I set an example other women could follow, and also gained respect for women's position in society. Who am I?

8) I was entirely self-taught and was one of the best scientific writers of the 19th century. I was also one of the first feminists. Who am I?

9) In the 19th century I submitted an essay on ferns to the Botanical Society of London, which was wrongly reported to be by my husband. He won membership of several scientific societies as a result. Who am I?

10) In 1933, I made the first X ray photograph of a protein. I went on to establish the chemical structures of penicillin and vitamin B12 and also won the Nobel Prize for Chemistry in 1964. Who am I?

11) My work to find the structure of DNA was taken over by three men who went on to win the Nobel Prize after my death in 1958. My studies were never recognised. Who am I?

7) Florence Nightingale 8) Mary Somerville 9) Margaretta Riley 10) Dorothy Hodgkin 11) Rosalind Franklin

Women have not only been held back in science, but in the arts too. For centuries, life in domestic slavery meant that we had no time to paint, write or learn a musical instrument. And anyway, because men were believed to be superior to women, it was thought that only they had the ability to be accomplished artistically. In 1888, the great painter Pierre Auguste Renoir said, 'The woman who is an artist is merely ridiculous.'

But women did paint, write, act and dance, finding ways around the restrictions on their artistic talents. Many of these women have been forgotten by the history books. For instance, you've probably heard of the famous diary of Samuel Pepys, but have you heard of the diaries of Anne Clifford, Margaret Cavendish or Mary Carleton, also from the same period?

Did you also know that Aphra Behn (1640-1689), best known as a playwright, wrote thirteen novels, thirty years before Daniel Defoe wrote what is usually referred to as the 'first novel' – *Robinson Crusoe*?

And did you know that the Royal Academy of Arts was founded in 1768 by two female – not male – painters, though a vote was later taken to exclude women from being members?

And did you also know that many of the great women Victorian writers had to publish their work using men's names, as writing wasn't thought a 'proper' occupation for women? Charlotte, Emily and Anne Bronte wrote as Currer, Ellis and Acton Bell, while George Eliot's real name was, in fact, Mary Anne Evans.

Quick Quiz

Q: What was unusual about the 1929 film 'Knowing Men' and who directed it?

A: It was the first 'talkie' (film with sound) and was directed by Elinor Glyn.

From directing, to script-writing, to acting, to producing, women have always played a large part in the film industry. But, as in many other fields, their achievements have largely gone unsung - purely because they were women! For instance, in early film-making days, female directors weren't credited, as it would drastically lower the box office figures.

Today in Hollywood, female directors such as Jodie Foster, Kathryn Bigelow and Jane Campion have more respect than ever before. And though there are now a few women in the top jobs in Hollywood, such as Lisa Henson, President of Columbia Pictures, and Sheri Lansing, boss at Paramount, it's still mostly men who have control over the money.

Lights! Camera! Action!

From the earliest days of film-making there have
been many excellent film scriptwriters, but it has
always been the (mostly) male studio executives
who have chosen which scripts to back financially.
As men decided which films were made, actresses
often found there was a lack of good parts for
women. For instance, films had the lead female
roles relying on the lead male character to save
them (like Julia Roberts' character in *Pretty
Woman*). Career women have been shown as evil
and grasping (like Sigourney Weaver's character
in *Working Girl*) and successful single female
characters have collapsed into madness in their
desperation to get a man and a family (like Glenn
Close's character in *Fatal Attraction*). The
powerful women in Hollywood now are trying to
put this right, but there's still a way to go
(compare the salaries of Demi Moore and her
husband Bruce Willis, for instance!).

Is TV any better? Research into TV programmes has shown that viewers normally see twice as many men on TV as women. The only time women are seen more than men is in sex scenes, as in two out of three of them only the woman's body is shown.

92

When it comes to presenting TV programmes, it seems it is more acceptable for men to be older or fatter than it is for women. How many middle-aged, wrinkly, overweight female presenters have you seen on TV? Now how many middle-aged, wrinkly, overweight male presenters can you think of? And women are still only thought suitable to present certain types of programmes, like children's TV, holiday or magazine-style programmes. How many women have you seen presenting serious political discussion programmes, compared to men? And can you think of any female game show hosts?

Because TV has been a male-dominated profession for so long, working conditions are difficult. People such as camera-operators, researchers, editors and directors often have to work long hours to meet tight deadlines, and at irregular times, too. As women still do most of the work at home, many find they can't commit to this kind of lifestyle, and choose to go freelance rather than holding on to permanent jobs. This means that few women reach positions of power in TV - even the successful Janet Street-Porter speaks of hitting a 'glass ceiling' - so it's still mostly men who decide which programmes are made.

Similarly, white, upper-class men have always been judges, in control of the courts and the legal system, so it's difficult for women to break into it and change attitudes. For instance, many women feel that rapists and sex-abusers should be dealt with much more harshly than often happens in our current male-dominated system. Male judges also often give women criminals worse punishments than they'd get if they were men. This is probably because most crimes are committed by men, so men often see a woman criminal as 'unnatural' and 'evil'.

The Daily Rag

women's page

Newspaper journalism is another area which used to be completely controlled by men. Female journalists are often afraid to write about 'women's issues' for fear of being seen as 'women's writers' rather than serious reporters, and so ending up being restricted in their careers. But newspaper stories have been written by male reporters and chosen by male editors for so long, that 'women's pages' written by women reporters and chosen by women editors help to right the balance slightly.

What we read in the newspapers affects what we think and how we feel, whether we know it or not. And it's not just what the newspapers report on that's important, but also how they do it. Journalists continually focus on women's appearances with comments like 'raven-haired mother of two' and 'Sally, an attractive sales-assistant'. Have you ever seen a man reported on in this way?

Peter Laganas, a muscular, blond, 45 year old coal miner, was today trapped down a coal-mine for six hours.

And why is there no male equivalent to a 'Page 3 girl'?

Many people believe that sexually explicit magazines and videos - whether for women or for men - are degrading and disrespectful, while many others enjoy such pornographic material, often sharing it with their partners as a part of sex. But women who enjoy these things complain that there are still many more adult videos, magazines and books for men than for women. And though people who disagree with pornography don't have to buy, read or watch it, they can't avoid the 'Page 3' pictures in daily newspapers, or magazines on newsagents' shelves. Many people feel that these pictures put across the message that all women are sex objects. They argue that this affects the way women are viewed and treated in society, and also increases the likelihood of violence against women.

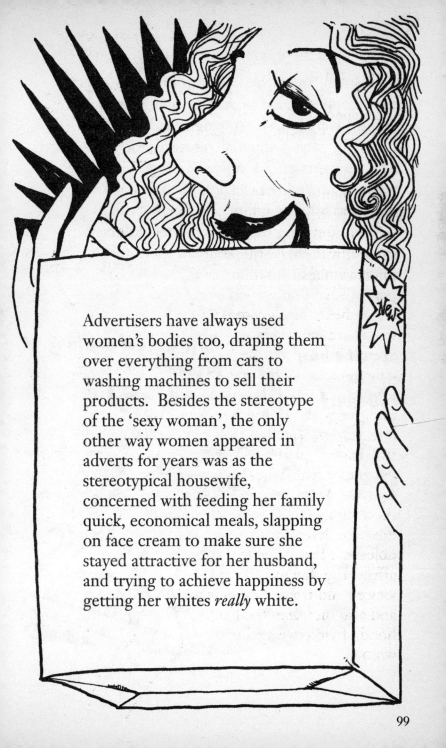

Advertisers have always used women's bodies too, draping them over everything from cars to washing machines to sell their products. Besides the stereotype of the 'sexy woman', the only other way women appeared in adverts for years was as the stereotypical housewife, concerned with feeding her family quick, economical meals, slapping on face cream to make sure she stayed attractive for her husband, and trying to achieve happiness by getting her whites *really* white.

As women became fed up with these images, they stopped spending money on the products being advertised, so campaigns had to change to reflect what women's lives were really like. Many adverts on TV now show men doing the washing up and the cleaning, female company directors holding important meetings, and women spending their own money on luxury cars. But there is still plenty of room for improvement …

Women's magazines enable women today to share ideas, experiences and problems. But most magazines rely on money from the manufacturers of beauty products to advertise on their pages and are restricted by the advertisers in what they can and cannot publish or say to women because of this. So these magazines can't publish articles on how to look beautiful without make-up, or how to stay young-looking without the latest anti-wrinkle cream, or else the companies would withdraw their advertising and the magazines would lose the money that they need to keep going.

Whether female or male, people have always enjoyed wearing make-up and experimenting with their clothing.

Until recently the fashion industry always exploited women more than men. But, as our society puts more and more emphasis on what we look like rather than what we are, more men than ever are developing eating disorders in their attempts to look 'perfect'. However, it has always been more acceptable for male models to look 'individual' or unusual than it has been for women; with distinguishing characteristics such as scars and lopsided features being thought of as sexy and desirable in men but not in women.

Most male models are expected to be tall and lean, but the male body shape does not go in and out of fashion in the same way as women's body shapes do. One year women are told that large breasts are in vogue ...

... the next year, flat chests are all the rage.

One year women are told to build up muscle and fitness, the next year the pale, wan 'waif' look is back in. Women in the West are seldom able to feel happy with their natural body shape.

Many women feel that they are being 'controlled' by fashion designers, beauty product manufacturers and the slimming product industry, who are deliberately making them feel unhappy about themselves.

Women feel that they have to spend their money on keeping up with the quick changes in fashion, or else face looking ugly and unattractive.

Today, advertisers are telling women to buy beauty products that can prevent the effects of ageing, but there are no such products on the market for men.

Why are women, and not men, being told that the natural process of getting old is a problem?

NO 27

The double standard of what is expected from women and from men has always existed in the area of sport. For centuries, women were thought to be the 'weaker sex' and discouraged from taking part in sport. They were expected just to watch men play it, then make tea afterwards or wash kit. Even today, boys are much more likely than girls to be pushed into team games at school, which is not just important for fitness, but also for teaching a sense of competition. Research has also shown that after marriage, men have more leisure time in which they can play sport, while women have less time of their own, and so do less exercise.

Heave!

Sportswomen today struggle against the attitude that men's sport is more exciting, accomplished and important than women's. Soccer, cricket and rugby are considered 'national sports', but when they're played by women, they have a poorer following, gain less TV coverage and aren't very highly thought of. All-female sports such as synchronised swimming often fail to be taken seriously at all! You may also have noticed that the male winners of major sports championships are paid more prize money than the female winners. And when sports commentators talk about 'the 400 metres' or 'the big match', people automatically assume they're referring to a men's, rather than a women's event.

Sports quiz

1　Where did the ancient Greeks get the idea from for the Olympic Games?

2　Which sport was Anne Boleyn passionate about?

3　In 18th century England, what sport was Elizabeth Stokes renowned for?

4　Who introduced betting on horse-racing?

5　What did Christina Willes invent in 1807?

6   What was New Yorker Gertrude Earle the first woman to do on 6th August 1926, in record time?

7   Who is the only athlete in history to hold the 5000m, 10,000m, half-marathon and marathon world records at the same time?

8   Which American basketball team did Lynette Woodward and Jackie White play for?

9   In 1980, what kind of race did Desiré Wilson become the first woman to win?

10   Which two Olympic sports are women-only?

Answers:

1 - From the women worshippers of the goddess Hera, who held their own female-only games as long ago as 1000 BC.

2 - Archery.

3 - Boxing.

4 - Queen Anne, in 1714.

5 - Round-arm bowling in cricket.

6 - Swim the English Channel.

7 - Ingrid Kristiansen of Norway.

8 - The Harlem Globetrotters.

9 - A Formula One motor race.

10 - Synchronized swimming and rhythmic gymnastics.

The first women to break into sport struggled not only with being excluded from all major competitions, but also with the clothing they had to wear - early women cyclists and tennis players had to cope with corsets and long skirts! But the barriers have been gradually pushed back. There are now women's football teams, women snooker players, jockeys, athletes, climbers, swimmers and karate grand masters.

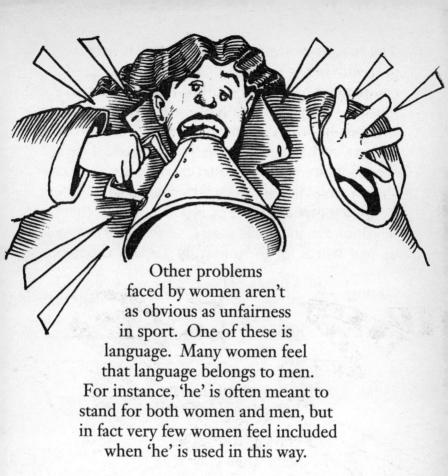

Other problems
faced by women aren't
as obvious as unfairness
in sport. One of these is
language. Many women feel
that language belongs to men.
For instance, 'he' is often meant to
stand for both women and men, but
in fact very few women feel included
when 'he' is used in this way.

Male words such as 'god' and 'actor' seem
more important than when bits are added on
to make the female versions, 'goddess' and
'actress'. And though some people try to avoid
using male words like 'chairman' or 'sportsman'
(by changing them to 'chairperson' or
'sportsperson') they only ever use
these for women!

Many women also find that they lack words to describe themselves and their lives and so need to create new words to solve this. For instance, to avoid labelling themselves as single or married, many women choose to use the new word 'Ms' instead of 'Miss' or 'Mrs', as an equivalent to the male term 'Mr'. The writers of the first dictionaries were men, so they only defined words that meant something to their own experience. For instance, why is there no word for a man who is a 'tart'? See if you can make up new words for the following 'female' experiences.

Getting your first period ----------------------------------

The female equivalent of a 'stud' --------------------

A word to describe your best girl friend
(other than the 'boy's' word 'mate') --------------------

The craving you get for chocolate when you're suffering from Pre-Menstrual Tension ----------------------

A woman who doesn't want to get married through her own choice ----------------

How you might feel if you'd been up all night nursing a screaming baby --------------

And just as women are held in low esteem by society, so are the words which describe them. For instance, 'bachelor' and 'spinster' are words used to describe unmarried men and women. But 'bachelor' suggests someone who goes out and enjoys life, and is single through choice, while 'spinster' suggest a miserable old woman left on the shelf. Similarly, 'bitch' is more familiar now as an insult than meaning a female dog, and even 'mother' is now used as a swear word.

Though women writers use language to speak out about women's experiences in books, books themselves often have the effect of restricting women's lives. Girls are given fairy-stories to read in which serving girls end up living happily ever after with the prince of their dreams, and comics filled with romantic stories. Boys on the other hand are given adventure stories, and comics filled with superheroes fighting and winning battles. Today, parents, teachers and publishers are much more aware of these stereotypes and try to break away from them as much as possible.

Some women feel that the writing in religious books, too, is manipulated by men to maintain their power over women. For instance, some Muslims claim that women have to cover themselves up to be good Muslims, but others say that there is nothing in their religious book, the Koran, to support this, while some Christians claim that men have deliberately interpreted the Bible to 'prove' that women are naturally inferior to men.

After all, Adam, if God created you after the animals, and you reckon you're superior to them, shouldn't I be superior to you, as I was created after you?

OK, Boss.

The age-old problem of violence against women is one that has not improved. All over the world, every day, husbands, lovers, fathers and brothers beat women who can't escape as they have nowhere to go. Women who are raped often find it too traumatic to go to court and face questioning not only about the rape itself, but also about their private lives. And half of all women who are murdered are killed by someone they know well, often after breaking off a relationship with them.

Even though women make up over half the world's population, it seems there is no safety in numbers.

SO WHAT LIES AHEAD?

Whatever you feel women's and men's roles in society should be, you can't deny that they are changing - and changing very quickly.
Women have more rights, more money, more independence and more opportunities than ever before, and men are having to adapt, whether they like it or not, to this new situation. Power and money are what make the world go round, and women are seizing these things with both hands.

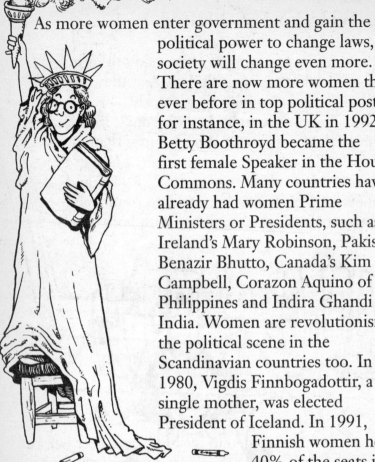

As more women enter government and gain the political power to change laws, society will change even more. There are now more women than ever before in top political posts, for instance, in the UK in 1992 Betty Boothroyd became the first female Speaker in the House of Commons. Many countries have already had women Prime Ministers or Presidents, such as Ireland's Mary Robinson, Pakistan's Benazir Bhutto, Canada's Kim Campbell, Corazon Aquino of the Philippines and Indira Ghandi in India. Women are revolutionising the political scene in the Scandinavian countries too. In 1980, Vigdis Finnbogadottir, a single mother, was elected President of Iceland. In 1991, Finnish women held 40% of the seats in parliament. And in Norway in the mid-1990s, Prime Minister Gro Brudtland and half her Cabinet were women, with women leading each of the country's three major political parties.

So many women can and do now vote that women actually hold the balance of power in the world. Governments can no longer ignore women's issues, as women's votes can make them rise or fall.

There are more women in business than ever before, and they aren't afraid of making money! Female entrepreneurs are seizing financial success, such as Anita Roddick, the founder of the Body Shop, and Ann Gloag, a former nurse who started a Scottish bus company and is now a self-made millionaire.

Women managers are changing attitudes to methods of working and conditions, and men in business have to deal with them if they want to stay in the game. And as women have more money, more and more opportunities open up to them.

Women today are trying for and achieving the heights of success in all walks of life.

Girls now outperform boys from GCSE to university level, and young women now account for more first time mortgages than young men.

Women are ordained as vicars in the Church of England and train as RAF fighter pilots.

The explorer Ffyona Campbell has walked around the world, and mountaineer Alison Hargreaves became the first woman to climb Everest without oxygen.

The best female athletes, such as Sally Gunnell, win Olympic gold medals and also win financially from prize money, sponsorship and appearance fees.

Helena Kennedy QC is one of Britain's best lawyers; the UK's Intelligence Service, M15, has had its first female boss in Stella Rimington; and Birmingham City Soccer Club has had a female managing director, Karren Brady.

Hanan Ashrawi has been the focus of world media attention as the spokesperson for the Palestinian delegation to the Middle East peace talks.

Female journalists such as Kate Adie appear on TV reporting from the frontline, women like Moira Stewart read the national news, and one of the top-earning TV presenters is a woman, Oprah Winfrey.

The earnings of top female pop stars, such as Madonna, now rival the wealth of their male counterparts, and female 'supermodels' earn even more than the top men.

Lynda La Plante has become one of the most successful TV scriptwriters, and Jennifer Saunders is a top comedian in both the UK and the USA.

Courageous women work in life-threatening situations, such as Pauline Cutting, the surgeon who worked in a refugee camp for a year and a half, under seige, with no electricity, no running water and very little food.

Women like Dr Sally Ride are even jetting out into space as astronauts - literally reaching for the stars! And of course, many of these women are mothers too ...

So will we ever see the day when we live in a 'matri-archy' and women rule the world? Would the world be a better place for everyone?

Or would women enjoy seizing power, oppressing and enslaving men?

Scientists are making rapid discoveries in the field of reproduction. For instance, women are now able to have children much later in life due to advances in fertility research. Doctors are now not only able to help infertile couples have a baby through test-tube treatment, they are also experimenting with ways to detect the sex of a baby before birth and also to create human life outside the female body (for example, with an artificial womb).

How will all these things affect the roles of women and men in society? Will one sex die out completely? Will men one day be able to have children themselves? Will the differences between women and men fade with time, until there is no longer any distinction between us?

We can't tell what the future will be like for our daughters and granddaughters, our sons and grandsons. But one thing's for sure - though the fight for women's rights certainly isn't over yet, it's less of a man's world today than it has been for a very, very long time.

WOOSH!

Further Reading

These books will tell you more about the ideas behind feminism and the development of the women's rights movement:

A Vindication of the Rights of Woman by **Mary Wollstonecraft (Orion 60)**
A shortened version of the original text, focusing on the key chapters.

Bluff your way in Feminism by **Constance Leoff (Ravette)**
A witty summary of the principles of the feminist movement.

(The following are suited to older teenagers)

Sweet Freedom: the struggle for women's liberation
by **Anna Coote & Beatrix Campbell (Picador))**

One Hand Tied Behind Us by **Jill Liddington and Jill Norris (Virago)**

Women of ideas, and what men have done to them
by **Dale Spender (Pandora Press)**

Outrageous Acts and Everyday Rebellions by **Gloria Steinem (Fontana)**
A collection of funny, hard-hitting and compassionate articles by one of America's leading feminists.

These books describe ordinary women's lives:

Women and the Arts/Women and Education/Women and Family/Women and Politics/Women and Wars/ Women and Work
by **various authors (Wayland)**

Out of the Doll's House by **Angela Holdsworth (BBC)**
A highly-readable account of life for women in Britain from the Victorian era to the present day, based on the memories of women who were especially interviewed for the TV series of the same name.

A Woman's Place by **Diana Souhami (Penguin)**
Describes the changing lives of different generations of British women, accompanied throughout by photographs.

Women at Work by **Sarah Harris (Batsford's 'History in Focus' series)**
Follows how women's working lives have changed over the years.

Solidarity: Women History Makers by **Anna Sproule (Macdonald)**
An informative book on the important roles women have played in shaping the world today.

The Women's History of the World by **Rosalind Miles (HarperCollins)**
A wide-ranging view of the hidden side of history for older readers.

In *Wild Swans* **(HarperCollins)**, **Jung Chang** tells what it was like for her grandmother, her mother and herself to grow up in China. The first chapter contains a detailed description of the practice of footbinding.

In *My Children, My Gold* (Virago) **Debbie Taylor** describes the lives today of seven single mothers in seven countries: China, India, Australia, Uganda, Egypt, Brazil and Scotland.

<u>You may not want to read the following books from cover to cover, but they are all interesting to dip into:</u>

Human Documents of the Lloyd George Era
by E.Royston Pike (Cullen & Unwin)
A collection of short extracts which speak vividly of girl's and women's work in the years before and during the First World War.

Women Assemble **by M. Glucksmann (Routledge)**
Chapter 4 describes what factory assembly line work was like for women between the First and Second World War, in their own words.

Parachutes & Petticoats **edited by Leigh Verrill-Rhys and Deirdre Beddoe (Honno Press)**
Welsh women's stories of life during the Second World War.

Truth, Dare or Promise **edited by Liz Heron (Virago)**
Different women's memories of their girlhood in Britain in the 50s (particularly *The Oyster and the Shadow* by Stef Pixner).

<u>Biographies and autobiographies:</u>

Look out for books on women who were pioneers in their field, such as Amy Johnson, Elizabeth Garrett Anderson and Marie Curie. You might also like to dip into *Seize the Moment* **by Helen Sharman and Christopher Priest (Gollancz)**, the story of Britain's first female astronaut, and *Battling for News: the rise of the woman reporter* **by Anne Sebba (Hodder & Stoughton)**

A Quiet Courage **by Liane Jones (Corgi)**
The heart-stopping true story of the brave women secret agents who risked their lives working for the Resistance in Nazi-occupied France during the Second World War.

Testament of Youth, **Vera Brittain's** autobiography **(Virago)**, is the famous account of a young girl's life from 1900 to the end of the First World War. The author was also a feminist.

Dale Spender puts the record straight with the other side of Samuel Pepys's famous story in her funny, thought-provoking book, *The Diary of Elizabeth Pepys*. This is what Mrs Pepys probably would have written, had she kept a diary!

Useful information:

The Fawcett Society
40/46 Harleyford Road
Vauxhall
London SE11 5AY
Tel no: 0171 587 1287
The Fawcett Society has campaigned for equality between women and men since 1866. The leading organisation for women's rights in the UK today, it works alongside other pressure groups and women's networks for greater equality and justice for women.

Womankind Worldwide
3 Albion Place
Galena Road
London W6 0LT
Tel no: 0181 563 8607
This charity is dedicated to helping women in developing countries help themselves, their families and their communities. Members receive a newsletter containing information on the issues affecting women all over the world and details of campaigns and activities in which you can participate.

The Equal Opportunities Commission
Overseas House
Quay St
Manchester M3 3HN
Tel no: 0161 833 9244
An independent body which seeks to promote and uphold the policies established by law regarding equal opportunities for all, and which investigates complaints of unfair treatment on the grounds of sex, colour, nationality etc.

International Women's Day
Since 1910, March 8th has been designated International Women's Day to celebrate the strengths and achievements of women all over the world. Around this time, watch out for TV and radio programmes, exhibitions you can visit, marches or campaigns you can join. You could also hold your own celebrations.

The United Nations Conference on Women
This high-profile international forum is a vital means of keeping up the momentum of pressure for women's rights. Attracting world-wide media attention, the fourth conference was held in Beijing in September 1995 and focused on the themes of Equality, Development and Peace.

Index